WIND ON THE SAND
The Hidden Life of an Anchoress

Pinions

 PAULIST PRESS *New York/Ramsey*

First published in 1980 by SPCK,
Holy Trinity Church
Marylebone Road
London NW1 4DU.

©Pinions 1980.

Published in 1981 by Paulist Press,
545 Island Road, Ramsey, N.J. 07446.

ISBN: 0-8091-2390-8

Library of Congress
Catalog Card Number: 81-80879

Printed and bound in the United States of America.

CONTENTS

Foreword	v
Preface	1
The Beginning	3
Following the Call	13
Prayer	22
The Testing and the Trusting	34
A Different Kind of Ladder	41
Involvement of a Different Kind	47
Joy is Deeper than Happiness	54
Existence of Freedom	59
The Our Father	63
Simple Prayer for People in a Busy World	68
Night Litany	73
The Religious Life	76
Epilogue	78

FOREWORD

Wind on the Sand is a fascinating book, which I enjoyed reading immensely.

This English anchoress writes with the astonishing matter-of-factness of so many people who lead a life of prayer. Prayer is her work, and she takes it as such. At one point she assures her director that she can, and does, "switch off" her prayer life when she is on leave. "I told him, 'Of course, leave is leave, and I begin again as soon as my leave is over.'"

In this, and in many things, she reminds me of the shrewd and simple St. Teresa of Avila who, when criticized for enjoying a good meal, said, "When I pray, I pray; when I partridge, I partridge!"

My favorite aspect of the book, and of the anchoress' life, is the running paradox involved in leading a life that partakes of the eternal, right here in funny old time. She corresponds with American astronauts; she prays for the workers who made the buttons of her dressing gown. She prays the Church's great round of prayers, and she prays for the people on television, and for all the people named in the *TV and Radio Times.*

All of these innocences would be merely charming were it not for her intelligent and unsentimental sobriety about the brief and eloquent voices that direct her life. Like most who hear such voices, she makes no universal claims for them. They wake her up. God utters to her a few words; she lets these words, and her interpretation of them, shape her life.

With her television, her cat, and her illness she is very much one of us. Yet she is not like us—because her work is more exacting than ours, and more important.

Annie Dillard

*This book is
dedicated to
a kindred spirit
in Christ*

Behold, I send an angel before thee,
to keep thee in the way,
and to bring thee into the place
which I have prepared.
Beware of him, and obey his voice,
provoke him not, for he will
not pardon your transgressions;
for My name is in him.
But if thou indeed obey his voice,
and do all that I speak,
then I will be an enemy to thine adversaries.
For mine angel shall go before thee.

                        EXODUS 23:20–23 *(Revised Version)*

PREFACE

THIS IS A TRUE STORY of the hidden life of an Anglican Anchoress, fully recognised by the Church of England, and known for her counselling by thousands of people of different creeds, all over the world. She works under a nom-de-plume so as to conceal her identity.

She is wholly given to God, nothing is held back for all is His, her life, her self, body, heart, soul, and spirit. She is a tool through whom God works.

It was about middle life, that she found Him in nature, first very forcibly in the Atlas mountains outside Algiers, and then in all nature and peoples.

About forty years ago she saw her first sand whirlwind blowing the red sand of Marseilles ever upwards and remarked at the time, 'some day I will write a book and it shall be called *Wind on the Sand.*'

Little did she know it would ever come to pass or be a religious book at that.

THE BEGINNING
Flee as a bird to your mountain

THE SUN had long gone down on its westward journey that November night and left behind darkness. I was glad to have an early night and very soon weariness got the better of me and I fell into a deep sleep.

Quite suddenly a 'voice' called my Christian name, as plain as if it was beside me, completely awakening me. The time was just after two o'clock. I got up and went to my father's room and said, 'You called me?'. He replied 'No'. So I went back to bed, quickly falling to sleep.

Suddenly the voice called my Christian name again and wakened me just the same as before, so I got up again and went to my father's room. But again he denied calling me, so I went back to bed only to be woken a third time by the same voice, so clear and so authoritative, that I repeated my journey to my father's room once more and said, 'But you did call me, I heard it each time, it woke me.' My father was furious, saying that I would wake my mother and telling me to go back to bed and stay there which I did and went back to sleep hearing no more. I never gave the episode another thought for many years.

I was not a real Christian in those days. It never occurred to me that it might have been a special 'voice', or a special 'call', and I dismissed the whole thing from my mind, thinking no more about it. Little did I know what was to happen in later years.

My parents often disagreed and quarrelled and when the situation at home got worse I became fed up with always having to try and make the peace. Also three of my brothers were killed tragically in a fairly short time. I took advice and left home. Having a car I found my own jobs, leaving each one for a better one, and I had my own rooms.

In 1939 came the second World War, stopping my job overnight. I had a favourite brother and we were like two peas in a pod. Both of us wanted to do the same thing, so decided we would try for the RAF. Bill passed all his exams (when he was seventeen) for Wireless Operator Air Gunner and was called up, when he was just seventeen and a half years old. I had a direct entry at Gloucester Training Camp as a WAAF officer (as we were called in those days) and was posted to Scotland where I worked with the 'Boffins'. My postings in England were short, about two years in all.

One day I received a telegram. Bill was missing during a Berlin raid. He was then a Pathfinder. He had been through so much that we had both become rather complacent. He had volunteered to take another's place that night. I can honestly say I almost went berserk. My grief was something no one could help me with. I hated everyone and, my goodness, one has to hate to the full to know the true reality of hate. I hated all English, Germans, and yes, I hated God. I hated Him most of all, if He existed. I neither knew Him nor turned to Him. Yes, I hated with all the hate there could be.

After some time I was posted to Northern Ireland, where in some kind of way I pulled myself together. From there I was posted to Algiers, North Africa, and after settling in, started work being in charge of WAAF who came a week later.

The beauty of nature soon came to my notice, especially the flowers. Every morning I had to go to work about five miles away and all the way in the distance were the Atlas Mountains with their enormous, rounded, coloured peaks, as if they had a curtain of haze heat cobwebs covering all their uncommon colours. These mountains hit something in me with a force beyond description. For one thing, I had hated God and never thought of Him, yet here in those unusual peaks, so very different from any other mountain tops I had ever seen, I saw Him. Morning after morning they drew me, riveted me, not as a person but as a Spirit. Day after day on my journey to work, there they were, so wonderful. Suddenly I saw in that colossal rounded mountain range the Almighty as Supreme Being. No one else could have put them there and I began to connect them with all the other beauties of nature that I saw, and I was never the same again. I knew nothing about the Trinity but was quite sure I had found God. It seemed as if a key had turned inside me.

I was in Algiers a fair time, and was to see those hazed peaks and my Spirit God many times together with all the other beauty. I picked a frangi-pangi flower and studied its beauty. Who could have made it but some Super Being? I never thought of any particular picture in my mind—to me it was Spirit. Later on I was not passing those peaks each day but they were still with me. I became compelled to learn more, to try and fathom out my new found wonder.

My work sometimes took me further away from Algiers, and if there was an SPCK bookshop I would browse through the books, instantly knowing which kind of book I wanted, but had no idea what faith I was following. I did not even know what the letters SPCK stood for and I went by the pictures and names on the covers of the books in the window! As things turned out it was the Anglo-Catholic Faith I was following, but I did not know it at that time. Work took me all over the Middle East and in Dar-es-Salaam I bought a Bible from the SPCK and set myself to read the whole book from beginning to end. I soon found it was one long, beautiful story, and that one had to read the Old Testament, in order to understand the New Testament.

After eight years I returned to England and then went to Europe until demobilisation when I went to stay with my godchild's family in Portsmouth. Of my own volition, I started going to Evensong in a nearby church.

All my life had been one of enjoyment. I loved good clothes, jewellery, dancing, parties, riding, pictures and the opera, in fact everything that any normal girl would enjoy. Quite suddenly while at Portsmouth, all desire for these things gradually fell away and I did not want them any more. I sold my jewellery telling nobody, continued to go to Evensong and kept the spirit of those mountains with me.

I want to make it quite clear there was no thought of a person or image in those peaks. In some way beyond words, it seemed as if the spirit of that massive rounded chain of mountain tops, swathed in the haze of the Algerian heat, was united with the spirit in me, and I knew it was God. It is the same today. I have no image of God but in some way beyond words or description His spirit continually touches mine and I know He is everywhere. In later years I told my director that the Spirit of God was everywhere and if one could cut the air, God would be in the cut.

During my travels all over the Middle East which took in Palestine as it was then, it was possible to see that country, including Jerusalem, as it was at that time. Of this I was very glad as it must be quite different now. After being back in England with my new found treasure, although the idea of entering a religious community never occurred to me, I decided to find myself a director. Having read many spiritual classics on the market at that time, my inner spirit was saying, 'Tell me more'.

I answered an advertisement and became the first warden of Canterbury diocesan conference and retreat house under Archbishop Fisher and his missioner. (Later he became Bishop of Zululand and died out there.) I asked him to find me a good director, and when the latter came to see me a terrible thing happened—I felt he was not the right man for me! So the missioner tactfully told him.

One day a monk from the Community of the Resurrection brought some retreatants to Canterbury. When I opened the door something flashed in me and I knew that he was the man. After an interview this monk became my director, and of my own free will I made my first confession. He is now dead but it was this monk who first perceived I had a religious vocation, but he never told me, and neither did it ever enter my own mind. All the books he suggested I had already read, including *The Cloud of Unknowing*, St John of the Cross, and Ruysbroeck. I did not find the retreat house work satisfying and I told my director so. Our relationship seemed to be no more than the director answering my questions and I found it rather wearisome.

One day he asked me whether I prayed and I replied: 'Once, as far as I know—in an aircraft about 1500 feet up flying on one engine over the Mediterranean Sea. The navigator came to the door and said, 'We've had it, chums, the other engine is going'. (The funny thing was I prayed for my parents who had been so unhappy and nothing for myself. But all that is another story.) Little did I know that all my reading and the tremendous 'draw' of my precious spirit mountain peaks were a form of prayer about which I had still told no one.

I now decided to change my director and try someone else when, at the next visit, he asked me if I had ever thought of becoming a nun. I was completely taken aback and replied, 'Good gracious, no'. He replied, 'I'm going to send you to a contemplative community'. I was not happy about this and tried to get out of it, but eventually an appointment was made for me to go and see them.

These people can be very persuasive and I entered a contemplative community as a postulant. My time as a postulant was not too bad. I found that the convent people were very nice. I still had not told anyone about my precious spirit mountains. They seemed to sacred to me, there were no words to express what I had seen and felt.

I do not know what happens to other communities or convents, but in mine you could not put yourself there. It all depended whether the convent would have you or not. It may be different now but in those days a person was not secure for quite a few years, and the final decision to stay rested with the community. This happened at each period up the ladder. It cannot be said that I learned much as a postulant, certainly nothing fresh, and I did not mind the silence.

After six months I was elected for clothing. These months as a postulant were perhaps less meaningful for me than they might have been for others. As a WAAF officer I had had a lot of discipline, had mixed with all kinds of people and races, and also held a great deal of responsibility together with charge of both officers and other ranks. The postulant work was mainly cleaning, washing up, and being a general dogsbody. I still had my inner secret untold.

I really did not mind if I was accepted by the community or not. Anyway the clothing did not signify anything final yet, so I let it take place and went into a week's retreat. It was between twenty and thirty years since I had first heard the 'voice'. During all those years I had never given it a thought. On the fourth day of my retreat I was awakened by exactly the same voice in exactly the same way. It just said 'Come'. It was then I remembered the previous voice I had heard so long ago. There was no difference in the tone and it came while I was asleep and wakened me in the same way. On the sixth night of my retreat the same thing happened again, and the voice said, 'Behold, I make all things new, that which I bear, so do ye'.

I never intended to be a nun. The thought had never entered my mind. My director had put me in the convent because he evidently saw something in me that I was not yet aware of, and in the convent I had come under their director. I still told no one of the spirit mountain peaks or the voice, although they were still very much alive within me. I began to realise that perhaps that first occasion I had heard the voice calling my name *was* a call from God, and I had missed it and did not recognise it. But for all this I asked myself whether I was now doing the right thing, especially as my presence in the convent was a result of being sent and not asking to be there. I asked myself what I had learned as a postulant. How to say the sevenfold official office, how to get used to silence—these were not difficult at all. In the war I had to keep secrets and this was a kind of silence. I certainly did not learn to obtain more knowledge, and also felt the convent prayer times were comparatively short. What I did not realise was that in some way which as yet I did not understand, I had been praying ever since I saw my mountain peaks and all the beauty of nature. The convent had given me books to read and something stopped me from saying I had read them all before—maybe fear of being thought a 'know-all'!

On the last night of my retreat the voice woke me again from sleep and repeated, 'That which I bear, so do ye'. After deep thought about these 'happenings' I decided to go ahead with the clothing. After all, being clothed did not bind me completely, but I still kept to myself all my precious things. I was duly clothed as a novice and joined the other novices.

Two weeks after clothing I heard the voice again. It wakened me the same as before, and repeated what I had heard during my retreat, 'Behold, I make all things new'. I did feel that being clothed actually made a difference. As a postulant one seemed 'apart', but wearing the same clothes (except for a white veil instead of a black) and saying the same prayers that go on with each garment, makes one feel more like a member of the community and that one has a goal for which to strive. But it also seemed that there was a difference between being a postulant when everyone was so nice, and being a novice. The whole thing changed. The 'niceness' was less frequent and the pressure was on. In the novitiate every personal aspect is pulled out and laid bare, sometimes before the whole community. One could be accused of things one had not done, given things to do with very little instruction, and told off if things were not carried out exactly according to how others did them. Tears were many, especially when being accused of something I had not done.

A novice has temporary vows, and the vow of Obedience in a convent is very great. On looking back I am sure I had passed all these stages, probably in my service career, and was now being put back instead of forward. As time went on I began to feel the dreadful weight of the clothes (especially as I am not quite five feet tall) and the daily work such as cleaning and cooking was monotonous. Prayer times I found much too short and re-reading books I found very irksome. In time, I became aware of lack of sleep because of the night office. I could never sleep when going back to bed after it, and I hung onto my mountain peaks for all I was worth. The voice puzzled me, not knowing if it was from God or just my imagination.

The time came when it had to be decided whether I should stay and go on to the next stage or leave. The community took the decision, then I was called in to discuss it. In my own mind there was a strong feeling that I wanted to lead a prayer life, but that the kind of life I was then living was not right for me and I constantly felt that I was being put back instead of forward.

It so happened that while discussions were in progress, a very wise priest whom I knew, came to the guest house for a few days. He saw me in the distance and asked to be allowed to see me. This was permitted, so he sent for me. I told him everything: mountain peaks, the voice, how I had come to that particular convent, what I had been through, in fact everything. I also told him that after five and a half years a prayer life seemed to be right for me, but not at that particular place. He asked me questions, and then said, 'It could be that you have a higher vocation'. I said I felt I was being kept back and not put forward. This priest monk asked me if I would put myself completely in his hands and I agreed. He then outlined what he proposed to do. He also told me that when I heard the voice again I should cross myself, then see if it was repeated.

It so happened that the night before I actually left, I stayed in a hut in the garden, and in the early morning the voice woke me by saying, 'My work shall not be done in big cities but at one point'. I immediately crossed myself and the words were repeated at once, again by the same voice. I told the priest what had happened, and he told me that the voice was from God. If it had not been, there would have been no repetition. Although I left the convent, I kept my temporary vows.

One day when I saw my new director, he told me he was going to train me for a life of prayer as an Anchoress, but he had to prove it was not escapism and it would mean keeping my vows and maintaining obedience to his direction. This I agreed to and we started by my going to see his Superior to be 'looked at'! After waiting for some time in the guest room, the Superior came in, walked round and round the table eyeing me at every turn, and left without a word. I was told later that he approved of the plan.

My first assignment was to a religious house which cared for unmarried mothers-to-be, the youngest being fifteen years. I only worked in the morning, the rest of the day being spent in prayer in my own room. My second assignment was to a home for old people, some of whom were very sick and I sat with the dying. My work now was only two hours in the morning, the rest of the day was spent in prayer in my very small room. The third assignment was to a house for maladjusted girls.

I must admit that my whole being rebelled against this next assignment. I begged to be given something else to do and left without agreeing, actually taking the next bus back to my current place of work. Then in the bus going back something very vivid happened. Straight in front of my face I saw before me the Crucified Feet, so clearly that the battle was won. I got off the bus and took the next one back, told my director what had happened and gave my submission. The Crucified Feet were so vivid before me I was able to see they were being held by only one nail. When I arrived back at the old people's home I was able to draw what I had seen. I told no one, only my director. It was my first vision.

> Oh! Jesus my Lord and Master,
> You have shown me a wonderful thing.
> But most of all You have humbled me,
> and cut away my pride.

FOLLOWING THE CALL
Far was the call and far I must follow

I NOW spent three and a half years under the same director, keeping my vows, until he decided I had definitely proved that I had a higher vocation and not a wish to escape from the world. For one further proof it was arranged that I should see the Father Superior General of the Community of the Resurrection and my file was sent to him. He wrote back saying he thought I had a vocation and arranged for me to see him. He died suddenly four days before the interview. My director then approached a former Abbot of Nashdom. I went there for the final interview, and waited in the big hall of the Abbey. I shall never forget the Abbot rushing round the corner from somewhere, down the rather long steps, scapular flying everywhere and eventually flopping into a chair facing me!

The first thing the Abbot asked me was: 'What will you do if this does not happen?' I replied: 'Try to find a job, of course.' He replied: 'All right, that will be all', and away I went! The Abbot wrote to my director, approving the plan, and it was decided that I should test my vocation in Walsingham. I was sent in secular clothes (for disguise) to see if I liked it.

There was one thing I would not do. Walsingham Shrine is a 'peculiar' which means it is not under the diocese or the established church as such. At the time I went to see it the diocese of Norwich was waiting for an appointment to the See. I told my director that I would not live this proposed life unless I was fully acknowledged by the Church, under the diocese and its bishop. For me it either had to be done properly and legally in the eyes of the Church or not at all. My director agreed and he had an interview with the Shrine Administrator and they suggested that I should come for one year to make sure everything was all right. He agreed and lent me a broken down hut with large cracks in the walls through which one could see daylight. When I moved in and made it ready the Administrator came to see it and as soon as he entered said: 'Oh, yes, it already has an atmosphere.'

The year went quickly. My Rule was made partly from the old 'Ancren Riwle', brought up to date, and partly from the rule of St. Benedict. There was now a new Bishop of Norwich, and I went to see him at the bishop's house in Norwich. All were now satisfied that I had this higher vocation and I returned to the hut and settled down to a life of prayer in earnest.

When the year in the hut was finished my director approached the bishop and asked him when he would be willing to profess me in this new branch and to make sure that I would be under the church in the diocese but not under the shrine church. The bishop was entirely willing to accept my vows to this higher vocation in a legal convent or in a parish church but not in the shrine church.

I was professed as an Anchoress in a legal convent on 26 November 1960 in five vows with life intention, to be renewed every year for five years. They were Solemn Perpetual Vows under the Bishop to whom I gave my first Obedience, and my second Obedience for small things I gave to my warden, a Cowley father, appointed by the bishop, and I was under the diocese and the diocesan directory but not under the Walsingham shrine. This meant I took no authority from the shrine neither could anyone interfere with me. A very kind benefactress had a cedarwood anchorage built for me on a piece of ground given by the shrine and it was enclosed. All was blessed by the bishop including a patch of unmade garden. The bishop then led me in the anchorage which was also blessed throughout, then I knelt down to receive his blessing. My warden then left me alone with the bishop. After a short talk the bishop also left and I was alone. Something inside me surged up and I knelt at my Prie-Dieu before the little altar, and holding out both arms to the Crucifix prayed aloud saying: 'My God and Creator, I am a disciple of Jesus, and have come to offer the sacrifice of my life as He offered His, according to Your Will. Keep me in Your Name that I may show forth Your Love to the whole world.'

The anchorage consisted of one small room which could be divided into two by a curtain, a very tiny cooking area, and a bathroom. The enclosed garden had to be made and I loved doing it. My Rule was tightened up when I moved into the anchorage. Exercise other than gardening was to be taken while it was dark, very early in the morning outside the enclosure, except on Sunday when I could take exercise when I wished. I was never to spend more than two and a half hours in prayer kneeling at one time. There were many other things, but everything was worked out by 'time' and I lived by the clock. Because this branch of the religious life is not attached to a community, it was necessary to have certain things which in the ordinary way would come from a community. A certain amount of money was allotted for my needs. I had to ask permission to keep other items, little things from my warden, larger ones from the bishop.

The first night I slept in the anchorage, I was awakened in the early morning by the voice in the same way as before. It said: 'Complete submission I require'. I crossed myself, and it was repeated. I replied, 'Lord, I desire to give You this submission. Grant me the grace to keep this disposition of heart and enable me to do it according to Your Will.' Then sleep came again.

At this period a realisation came that I had been praying for a long time and had come a considerable way in prayer since I first saw the Spirit Creator in the Atlas Mountains. I was desperately happy with a quiet inner happiness and marvelled at the way God had brought me to my present position.

After a fortnight the tragedy happened. I suddenly had some back trouble. It became worse so my warden allowed me to see a London consultant, who told me I had two progressive incurable diseases. Nothing could be done but they would make life liveable for me. I returned to the anchorage and at once completely went to pieces. I saw my whole world and future falling before me, and self-pity swept over me. This all lasted four days and nights. It took me that time to accept it and to come to terms with it. I pulled myself together remembering that the hospital had said they would make life liveable for me and started to think about how I could use this blow. Had I not said that I gave my Creator complete submission? I decided, or maybe was shown inwardly, what to do. From that time on I would unite my suffering to Christ's sufferings on the cross, for Him to perfect, and offer them to God for all people in the world who rejected pain. In this way my suffering would become just a tiny pin-prick in the help of the redemption of the sin of the world. Had this back trouble come earlier, profession would not have been permitted, but I can honestly say that I neither felt nor had any knowledge of it until a fortnight after profession. The bishop took all this into account and, with my warden, decided it was the work of God, and the reason would be made known in His good time.

Early in the morning after I had accepted the trouble, I was wakened from sleep, and while still sleepy my mind instantly saw thousands upon thousands of the tops of completely bare skulls. There was no place without them. At once the voice came: 'Implore My Mercy for sinners, the heart must be a furnace of love for sinners.' As usual I crossed myself, and although the skulls disappeared, the voices repeated the same words again. This command I have carried out ever since. The extraordinary thing about this 'seeing' was that the skulls were thousands upon thousands of just the bare white tops. Also it was the first time that the voice had come with any vision. My first prayer for these bare skulls was immediate: 'I implore Your Mercy for sinners, my heart must be a furnace of love for sinners. Oh Lord, make it so.' I still say this prayer regularly. My answer was spontaneous, and to this day anything God shows me or tells me to do is just as spontaneous.

I was not allowed to see people for counsel for three years. During that time it was necessary to become completely one with my own lifestyle, and learn a great deal about the Bible. Above all I tried to carry out my Creator's instructions and use my back pain for others and learn to live with it myself.

I love the Bible, but it must be read in short passages at a time, about six to eight verses, and it must be read *in depth*. This is very important if it is to be understood and enjoyed. One also needs a very good commentary. It is excellent to read the same passage in several different editions. The Bible that I have found so good is the Revised Standard Version Study Bible distributed by Eyre and Spottiswoode. It is well set out and has extremely good notes. I believe the Bible to be the original Holy Word of God given to those who wrote it for the benefit of all Christians and peoples down the ages. It is one long, beautiful story, and one cannot understand the New Testament if one does not understand the Old. The Old Testament is not in chronological order but once understood it is not difficult to see it as a whole. Read in depth and understood, one finds the characters come to life, one sees why the various things happened and down the ages to the birth of Our Lord and why that precious birth, the saving gift from God to man, had to take place. I think we should all reflect on this subject. Time changes, but the Word of God as given to us for all time does not change, and if the Bible is read with prayer, the true meaning illumines one's mind. It is good to understand it in its own age by taking oneself back to that time. I use the following prayer before all holy reading: "Oh, Holy Spirit of God, open my mind and show me what You want me to learn in this, my holy reading'. In this way, any holy reading is approached in the correct way. Is not history repeating itself to a great extent today? We still have war in Syria and the Lebanon!

For years I read the Bible and what I read was all familiar to me, but it was not until I changed my reading habits that the Bible suddenly came to life, and what I had seen sliding on the top of my mind became quite different in meaning in the depth of my mind. I marvelled at the difference, often thinking: 'Why did I not see these things before?' They were known but dead, now they are known and so alive. I was humbled to know that I could be so stupid.

We must now return to the anchorage. During these first years I gradually learnt the depth of the vows I had taken and what they meant. I made the garden and before starting work I always used the following prayer:

> God planted a garden and there He put man whom he had formed, to dress it and keep it.
> Oh blessed Jesus our Lord and God, who in a garden bowed Yourself to the work of man's redemption, and in a garden revealed Your risen glory, grant me to labour that the fruit of Your Redeeming Love may be shown through me in the beauty of holiness to all men.

I still use this prayer when attending to plants in my room. In recreation time I made church linens and did art work, chiefly Christmas cards for a market in America. These all bore a message of some kind. My letter writing was limited to about six people, apart from my Bishop whom I saw once a year, and of course my warden.

At the very beginning of life in the anchorage I had a feeling that I had been praying for a very long time and had not known it, and that I was much further on in my prayer life than I knew. I also felt the nearness and guidance of God. I can honestly say no human being ever converted me or gave me any human help at all except my bishop. From the time I realised the Spirit of God in those Atlas Mountains, God Himself seemed to 'take over' my inner life in His own way and time. It was only when I started my new life seriously that this realisation became for me a reality.

One point of my Rule states that I live 'in Christ separated unto the Gospel of God, so as to give Him Contemplative Prayer, Praise and Adoration on the one hand and ceaseless Intercession for all people'. Later, when I became ill, the following was added as my vocation, 'and an offering of my suffering, on behalf of His Body the Church and the whole world, on the other'. It must always be remembered that when Christ's Body, the Church, is mentioned it means two things—it does not mean just the church building and its clergy alone. It means that the Church and the people make up the body of Christ. The Church cannot work without the people, and the people cannot really live without the Church. They may exist but just to exist is not real living. It takes the people and the Church to become a real living body.

After about three years I was allowed to see a few people who wished to see me for counsel, and to write more letters to those who needed help. It was also the start of my writing religious poetry. It was found that if I enclosed a poem with my letters to people, they received great help from it; they sometimes remembered it better than the letters. The words came to me without any effort.

It was while I was sitting at my table to write one day that, quite suddenly, I had an instant clear vision of the Crucified Head—the top and half way down the eyes. It was instant and brief and showed quite clearly that Christ wore a whole cap made of thorns, not just a crown. The thorns were vicious and all over the head and were digging into the forehead. The blood was running down from them to the eyes beyond description, and it was running in close lines in such a way that one could never imagine it so, and it had a great effect upon me both then and afterwards. I am always inwardly very humbled by this vision which was really beyond imagination. There was no voice and it happened at half past eleven in the morning when I was fully awake and only lasted a flick of a second. It was something that I could never forget.

Some months later my benefactress came to see me and brought with her two large books by James Tissott, an artist who lived in France from 1836–1902. He visited Palestine twice and wrote the Life of Our Lord with wonderful illustrations throughout, and finished them in October 1886 when he was eighty years old. He gave a copy of the two volumes to a Mr. Gladstone in 1897 and wrote his message in Volume 1 in his own hand and signed it. The text of the books unfortunately is not always correct but the etchings and paintings are superb. I had not seen these books before and on the title page of the first volume, under the official heading, was the part of Christ's head exactly as I had seen it in my vision. The picture proved that what I had seen was exactly the same and I was quite shattered. Here was proof that someone a century before me had seen what I had seen.

The five years in temporary vows were now over and the time had come to confirm my vows for life. My warden, the bishop, and the Shrine Administrator had a conference about my health. Then I was asked what I wished to do. I now had more illness and one leg had been made straight by an operation at the knee joint which had given way through my bone trouble. I told them I wished to consecrate all illness I had at that time together with any in the future. They all agreed and my five Solemn Perpetual Life Vows were confirmed in the same convent as before on 1 March 1965. My own bishop received them, and present also was a second bishop, the Father Superior of the Society of St John the Evangelist (the Cowley Fathers), who also acted as my warden, as my previous warden had gone to America on sick leave.

My bishop, having received and confirmed my vows, said, 'I authorise you (giving the Office Book) to recite the Divine Office as permitted in the Canonical Hours of the Church. In the Name of the Father and of the Son and of the Holy Spirit. Amen.' The bishop then changes the Anchoress' crucifix. The document is then signed, held up for all present to see, placed on the altar, then later attached to the Professional Deed.

> Oh! my Father and my Creator
>   indeed far is the 'Call'.
> Give me the grace and the strength
>   to 'follow' as far as You desire.

PRAYER
And Jacob dreamed there
was a ladder set up on earth

WHAT IS PRAYER? It is the lifeline through Christ from man to God. Through the Holy Spirit, we have part or whole union with the Creator, here on earth while we are finite beings, meaning we are all in a limited, bounded state in this life on earth. God the Creator is infinite, meaning not limited or bound in any way whatsoever. He is Spirit, and perfection in everything. We offer prayer through Christ, because He is the link who, on the human side, perfects prayer, and on the divine, passes it on to the infinite God in perfection, and so the lifeline of prayer from people to God is formed. It is always difficult for people to believe and understand something that cannot be seen, so what is it that makes everyone want to pray?

It may be some tragedy or great distress (although these things can have other results) or something very beautiful. I quote the American astronauts with whom I have had much exchange during their training and moon flights. They practically all say it would be impossible to go to the moon, or see the world from high orbit and not believe in a Super Being. Prayers have been said by them in orbit and on the moon. They have been drawn to prayer by sheer beauty and wonder. Sometimes before they start, the astronauts have been very conscious that they are putting themselves into the hands of God, and what happens to them on their mission rests with Him.

To me the realisation of God first came in the Atlas Mountains and then in the beauty of nature which stirred my whole inner being. The flowers growing everywhere were absolutely breathtaking, and I saw in them such beauty and wonder that could not have been put there by man. When I picked the frangi-pangi flower and thought much about it, I saw the Spirit Creator. Who else could have made such beauty?

I have known people who have never prayed before, pray at the point of death. The need or wish to pray moves people in many different ways. We all have a very precious interior with all our faculties, such as the inherent power of the mind and our senses to perceive and understand, a mental alertness. These things are all inward things; but if we do not use them they stagnate. An artist who does not paint for some months, finds that when he starts to paint again his work is sub-standard, because his senses and artistic power have been dormant. For someone who has never prayed there is always something that touches the inner self and sparks off the feeling of the need to pray, even if it is only being near death.

People these days often have strange names attached to types of prayer. Transcendental Meditation is one. Why 'transcendental' when it is just ordinary meditation! It is not a supernatural prayer and one does not come into it immediately. There are lots of different types of prayer on the ladder of perfection but I am only going to mention a few, so that people will not get muddled. The name of a type of prayer does not make a person pray, any more than the habit of a nun! One does not need to be a monk, a nun, or priest to live a life of prayer. All life can be turned into prayer.

There are two things which are absolutely necessary for prayer. First, a complete and unwavering faith in God, as Spirit and Creator of all, His Son Christ, in his divine and human nature, together with the Holy Spirit who is the source of all our inner being, and without whom we cannot pray. These things are not myth, but mystery, and there is a very great difference in the meaning of these words.

Secondly, there must be no doubt for doubt is the devil's gold against us and the better we pray and the nearer we get to God, the more will the devil put on his pressure. This must be stamped on at once. Our Lord said: 'Get you behind me, Satan'. We can say or think the same kind of thought, or we can say 'drink your own poison, Satan' or some short sentence. We must always remember as well that the devil uses his own spirits in various disguise. These we must learn to deal with also; they attack us in all kinds of disguise, even sometimes in other people.

So we see how prayer can start in anyone, even myself, who had never bothered to pray, never been conscious of a Super Being until I saw my mountains. Once natural beauty had turned my heart to God I found myself continually raising my heart to God, without words but in thought. That is prayer in itself. So my foot was on the ladder. I never have had any doubt. I only wanted to find out more. I wanted knowledge, and this was obtained by reading, first the Bible and then other books, not on prayer but spiritual classics.

I have spoken about my book finding. I, and people who have dealt with me, firmly believe this book finding was the work of God's guidance through the Holy Spirit who had been sleeping within my inner being since my baptism. So seeking became very important in my first learning, and the more I studied the stronger became the knowledge and the desire to pray. At this point most of my prayer was the lifting of my heart to God in thought and a very sincere certainty that He was Creator of all, that He was spirit in everything and everywhere. I have never once, even in those early days thought of God as anything else but spirit in everything and everywhere. Having researched much I have understood Christ's divine and human nature, and the work of the third person, the Holy Spirit. From early days the Holy Trinity and his work have been very clear to me. People who have looked at some of my work and know me, all believe that God Himself through the Holy Spirit has shown me this knowledge and understanding.

I did not remain in this early type of prayer for long. I began to feel the need to pray with words and to meditate on some Bible or book passage that I had read.

MEDITATION

Meditation is an interior movement which makes a person want to reflect in deep absorption of thought and prayer, aloud or in silence, directed to Christ alone, or through Christ to God. Some people need to read a short passage in the Bible or spiritual book to start them off, but I never had to do this. I found no difficulty in praying in my own words—making up my own prayers. I could be alone with God for the whole two and a half hours allowed by my Rule, kneeling in prayer without any difficulty. Subjects came to me without any trouble and I prayed about them in my own way and also gathered up the fruits God gave me. Although I did pray kneeling at that time, for the benefit of others may I say it is not necessary always to pray kneeling. One can pray in any position, anywhere and at any time. I always called upon the Holy Spirit before starting, such as 'Oh! Holy Spirit of God show me the words I should pray, and speak them through me; also illuminate my mind as to what I should learn'. I had been warned about distractions, but although most people have to suffer the devil's provocation, I have never been bothered with distractions at any time. If people are bothered by distraction during prayer, it is good just to drop them from the mind at once like a stone into an imaginary pool of water, and carry on as if they have never existed.

A person who wishes to meditate should seek in reading (not necessarily at the prayer time), discover the depth of what it means in meditation, then pray about it or for it. Our Lord said: 'Seek and you will find, knock (pray) and the door will be opened for you'. The knowledge one gains is put away and stored in one's interior, but not forgotten. My seeking seemed to come directly to my mind and I understood a great deal from the beginning.

At about this time I was wakened again early one morning by the voice, exactly the same voice as always. 'All are made in the image of God'. I crossed myself and it was repeated and as usual I fell asleep again. I used these words for my meditation later that morning, during which time I thought about the word 'image'. I wondered how this could be since I was sure God was spirit. I prayed to be shown more about this word and spent all my meditation time on it. After some time of praying in words, quite suddenly the answer flashed within me. The word 'image' meant nature, God's nature, and Christ was the image on His human side showing us God's nature which was how we were to live. It was Christ who was the image of God's nature and He was showing people God's nature and how people were to imitate that nature as far as possible.

Meditation of this kind is definitely a feeling directed towards God and His Love, not temporal love as most people think of love, but a spiritual love which is deep in one's interior, a realisation of God's love for His creation, including all mankind, and a response from mankind back to God, in which one uses new faculties and senses that have been dormant through lack of use and probably not even known to exist. This was a great wonder to me and I used to say, 'Father, I thank You' many, many times, and soak up the wonderful mysteries of God and Christ, using without any effort the faculties and senses as God directed, and waiting upon the Holy Spirit to convey to me anything else I ought to know. Some people stay in this ordinary meditation for many years and do not move on to a higher form of prayer.

I later began to feel this kind of meditation was no further use to me. Having told my director this, he advised me to stop and see what happened when I started to pray. This is important because when one finds this ordinary kind of meditation is not necessary, it is a sign that prayer is going to develop into some higher form, probably into the realms of contemplation, and so we come to the Prayer of Quiet.

THE PRAYER OF QUIET

Union with God in this type of prayer is usually quite short but very wonderful. The more fine the movements of prayer of this kind, the more divine it is. It is true that the more a person does not know the obscurity, suppleness and the knowledge of what one does in this form of prayer, the more divine it becomes. There are no words to express it. I found this to be true and God gave me the understanding that at intervals I was very near to Him; it could be said I felt Him. I would inwardly see something of the beauty (for want of a stronger word) of the Creator and His purpose, the meaning of God, Christ, and the action of the Holy Spirit, and I would be in the Divine Arms and even quietly utter just short words aloud, such as, 'My God I am not worthy' or, 'Oh! I believe, take from me all that displeases You', or, 'You have the whole of my faith' or, 'I love You' or, 'Oh my God', in fact anything that the Holy Spirit moved me to speak in answer to what the divine Creator was giving me.

When I was in this type of prayer there were long or short periods when I was so wrapped in the divine I did not speak at all, but it was not difficult to know that mysteries were active inside me. It acted as a further drawing near to God, and He to me. If there is but a lifeless vacuum within, then there is no prayer at all, and when this happens one must temporarily return to a lower form of prayer. This never happened to me and I became aware of much spiritual fruit. It made me feel very humble but also very happy. It also made me understand what a speck I am in God's sight and it very much heightened my own faults in contrast to God's perfection and the beauty of His holiness. How little my whole love was against His tremendous Love for me, and how soiled against His purity.

RECOLLECTION

Again I did not stay many years in this first mystical and supernatural prayer. From this God led me on to recollection; that is recollecting God or Christ at different times of the day. I have never experienced the 'darkness', or the feeling that God had deserted me, that some people talk about and call the 'dark night'. I always get an intuition when something is going to happen to me that will not be pleasant, but not exactly what it will be, or when it will happen.

I had an intuition, while not at prayer, that something was going to happen, and in roughly two months from that time I became very ill and had to go into hospital. These things never disturb me. Since my first illness I always take them as God's will and my faith was always so strong that I knew God would show me what to do with whatever was to happen. I went into hospital, and was told I had kidney failure in an advanced degree. It was inoperable and a kidney machine would not work. I asked and was told my expected life length, which has already passed! This told me God had more work for me to do on earth.

When I came home I knelt down and directly went into the Prayer of Quiet. I realised that God already knew all about it, and almost at once I was to use it, and all the pain I ever received, for all people who cannot accept suffering and so often say, 'Why should this happen to me?' I was also to use it for all world suffering. This I have done ever since by uniting my pain and physical suffering to the suffering of Christ on the Cross, for Him to perfect and pass on to God, for all suffering people whatever religion or none, and so just become a tiny 'pin-prick' in union with Christ in the redemption of this poor sick world.

The next morning I was wakened again from deep sleep by the voice which said: 'That which is done through Love, with love, never hurts'. As usual I fell asleep again. After my first illness, nothing in this way ever worries me. I always accept and put all into God's hands and am quite happy.

My recollection increased, I found I was never out of it. When sitting in a chair I give some prayer for those who made it, when going through a door, I will ask that the will of God may be done for all undergoing operations at that moment. When putting on my dressing gown I will pray briefly for those who made each part of it, even the buttons. I told my director about this and he asked me if I could switch off when on leave. I told him, 'Of course, leave is leave, and I begin again as soon as my leave is over'. My director told me this kind of recollection was of God and called 'infused' recollection, meaning something one cannot give oneself. Now I have done it for years. In fact I can do three things at once all day and no one would ever know. At God's appointed time He led me into 'infused contemplation'.

CONTEMPLATION

There are many kinds of contemplation and if one desires, even if working in a busy world, one can teach oneself to contemplate, but infused contemplation is only given by God to whoever He desires to give this grace. Humbly, I can say He has given it to me and it is something very wonderful. It is something that just cannot be put into words, because it is being continuously so near to God and 'seeing' clearly all things supernatural. One is always in prayer and there are no words to describe this precious state. What can be said is that one sees sin very clearly especially in one's self, and understands how sin hurts God and puts another nail into the hands and feet of Christ, and it makes one feel great sorrow. It is such a powerful form of contemplation that I found that it gave great suffering. I had had a glimpse of the Creator, His love and work, and there is suffering because of being in a finite state. There is the boundary of not being able to get any nearer the infinite. There is the clear knowledge that my finite spiritual love cannot equal the Creator's infinite spiritual love and that is a suffering in itself.

I wish to explode a myth here. People are apt to think contemplation is done in long periods on one's knees. This is not so. It is done anywhere, doing any work, at any time. For a busy working person who wishes to practise ordinary contemplation, after making a short morning oblation, the work becomes the prayer. This fact often disappoints the people wanting to join religious orders, as they find it is not what they had imagined it to be.

It had been about eighteen months since I was awakened by the voice, then one morning it came again while I was asleep and wakened me saying, 'Come up higher'. I crossed myself and it was repeated, so I answered, 'Show me how Lord', and went to sleep again knowing that I would be shown.

I think it should be said that I hardly ever consciously dreamed, perhaps once in two or three years, and I never judge any of the phenomena I have spoken about. I have always told a person of more knowledge of such things, to see if they are of God and not of my imagination. They are so precious that I never want to describe them to anyone. I have never asked for them or any other favours from God. I would not be making them known now if this account was not being written in obedience, in order to help other people. What I and others feel is that God meant to have me for Himself, to do what He directed, and to become His tool through which He could work with the Holy Spirit. That is why my directors gave me so little guidance, except when I asked. This I did whenever anything out of the ordinary happened. I have never trusted my own interpretation; in fact I have never thought of doing so, and never dwell on what I have heard, unless it is something I am told to do at once, then I do it and continue. Otherwise I wait until it is God's good time to let me know the answer.

INTERCESSION

I have often been amazed at the way some people pray their intercessions. They make long lists of intercessions until there are so many lists they cannot manage. I have never done this. I believe God already knows the people I am going to pray for, so why waste time telling Him all over again! Some of my intercessions for people are done in blocks. Take for instance the columns of deaths in any daily paper. I glance at the whole list and I pray for them all at once, 'according to the will of God'. I understand so clearly how Christ could see the whole of the world when tempted by the devil. In supernatural prayer one can see so much at one time in the mind, and very sharply. Being or working in a busy world gives ideal chances for intercessory prayer, and my prayer life developed quickly once I had been shown by God Himself what He wanted of me.

I once told my first director in the early days, that somehow I did not see people just as people, but that deep down in my interior I saw them all as souls, and that it was only the outside of me that saw the actual people. It is difficult to explain, but it is as if I saw them from their interior outwards. I found this extremely useful, because it encouraged my prayer for them at once whether I knew them or not.

The radio and television are ideal for intercession. I am allowed a television, and every single person living or dead that I see on it daily receives prayer. It is the same with the radio. Every named person in the *TV* and *Radio Times* has daily prayer. A daily newspaper is an excellent thing for intercessory items for prayer. I do not have to read it from page to page—the headlines tell me the basic information. If something demands prayer, then I will read the whole article. In my younger days in the WAAF I travelled overseas a great deal. This I now find very useful, because I know the countries and peoples and this enables me to understand better now why there is trouble in some countries between certain peoples. I pray for all people whatever their religion or needs. Another marvellous thing is that my previous life, with all the experiences I had, fits into a kind of mosaic pattern to make my present life.

One does not have to know people personally to intercede for them. I intercede for all peoples and countries and I leave it to God to guide me. I myself am just His tool through whom the Holy Spirit works, according to the will of God. Nothing is my own, even though I pray the words and make up the prayer. All is from God, and oh! how I love my Creator.

One last thing on the subject of intercessions: don't forget that the *Our Father* can make a wonderful intercessory prayer, and also parts of the Psalms.

Oh! my Father You have implanted Your nature within me and shown me many things.
If it be Your Will, in the Name of Christ, give me the strength and wisdom always to make these things known to others, when You desire it, even if they are like dust upon the earth.

THE TESTING AND THE TRUSTING
The Flame of the Fire does not shine
but I know my Redeemer lives

I HAVE SAID in an earlier chapter that I received intuition about things that were going to happen to me personally. For some months I had had an intuition that something was going to happen. It must have been about four months later when I became ill again and had to go to my London hospital and was kept in, as I had a fever. These were kidney fevers of which I was to have many. The hospital thought that Norfolk was too far away and that I ought to be nearer to them, and have someone to look after me. When I was better one of my consultants came and told me I must leave Walsingham and live nearer the hospital. This was a terrible blow to me, for I had lived my life, loved the anchorage and its garden, and my life had progressed in the nine and a half years I had been there.

The place for me to go and live in order to be near my own hospital was chosen, and I was given four days after getting back to Norfolk to move all my belongings for one room, and get rid of the rest. It was all so sudden and unexpected, I really had no time to think. Here my hospital was very wise because if I had time to think, I believe I would rather have died than moved, and nobody knows the volume of tears that were shed in the dark of the first night of the four days back at the anchorage. Self-pity, of course!

All at once God came to my help. Suddenly the 'voice' I had heard some months before said, 'That which is done through Love, with love, never hurts'. It was the first time I had thought of those words again since I had heard them. Then another memory came: had not my Creator asked for 'complete submission' by the 'voice', and had I not already given that submission? Did I not know that God knew what He was doing with me, even if I did not. Oh! fool that I was to weep those tears! From that moment on, they stopped. Now there was work to be done and that had to be done quickly. The hospital had already been in contact with my bishop, as I am not permitted to move residence without his permission except to go to my hospital for visits. The hospital had also contacted the new residence. I obtained the help of the very generous gardener at Walsingham. He produced tea-chests and helped me pack enough for my one room and my books; the rest I gave away. He and I packed those things too, and I left them all with my helper to send the various tea-chests to their destinations by road service. I prayed that God would bless the people who were to receive them.

Before leaving the anchorage I would like to remember two things. First, one Sunday afternoon when I was taking my exercise, a car-load of Americans stopped and asked me the way to the Shrine. Early that evening, I was kneeling at prayer within the Shrine in what I called 'St Joseph's niche'. This was a darkish corner running back from the small chapel of St Joseph within the Shrine. The Americans came to look at the little chapel, a mother, father and two children. One of them suddenly saw me kneeling at prayer in the niche and said: 'Look, they even have a nun's statue'. They all came over and bent down to inspect the supposed statue. They did not recognize me from the afternoon meeting and I never moved a muscle. 'Isn't it wonderful', one said. 'So real, all the clothes too, I wonder if it's wax', said another, and the lady bent down and tweaked my nose with her finger and thumb. This did it; even the well-trained Anchoress broke into a broad smile. 'Oh! my God, it's alive', said the lady. 'No', said the man, and tweaked my nose from the other side and I am afraid my smile became silent good laughter! Never have I seen a family move away so quickly.

The second thing was that my garden became a bird sanctuary and I learnt a great deal about birds. They had no fear of me, and when sitting in my garden reading sometimes in the summer, a thrush would come and sit on my foot and sun its outspread wings. When I had my breakfast I would leave the anchorage door open in the summer and the birds would come right inside and peck up the crumbs round my feet. They had no fear of me at all. These birds also brought their families when ready. I later found out that this bird trust was because of my silence. Once I spoke to them all went like the wind, and I praised God for the trust of his creatures. Providing I remained silent they had no fear of me in any way and I learned a great deal about their ways.

After nine and a half years, the happiest years of my life, the move had to be and I had to trust. This was God's test. I arrived back at the hospital on the evening of the fourth day, and moved into my new home the following day. It was a terminal hospital but some of those not yet in an advanced state had single rooms, and later would move up to the hospital part. But in my case I should be moved to my own hospital. I had one room and did not come under the hospital medically, having my own general practitioner, and I kept my own drugs from my own hospital to which I could go by private taxi when they needed me. The scheme worked well, but I soon found out I could not work my ministry there. I tried desperately hard to live my life there, but it was no use. It just was not possible to do my work at all. After two and a half years, the unhappiest of my life, my own hospital noticed something was affecting my health and asked me about it. I told them, and it was agreed that I should move again.

During the time of looking for a new suitable place, a lady whom I had helped offered me a room in her house in Worcester. This was put to my London hospital. Some of my consultants said yes but one said it was too far away. In the end, after I had had my tests, he agreed providing I came to London whenever they wanted me. This I promised to do. So I went to Worcester and it has been my one-room anchorage ever since.

It was very hard to leave my Norfolk anchorage where so much prayer had gone to God. But I trusted God that His Will would be done by me and in me in whatever He did with me. Also I am a great believer that in the end, 'All things work together for good, for those who love God'. My own life is proof of this belief.

My room has a small lobby and it is bright. The bathroom is very near, and the whole house has a Christian atmosphere. I go to my hospital by car lying on the back seat whenever they want me. It is my belief that all this happened to bring about the 'happenings' of later years, of which at that moment I had no knowledge. The future would not have come to pass, I feel sure, if I had not gone through with it. My benefactress saw to all the moving of my furniture, and she herself kindly fetched me in her car. I must admit my heart beat double time as we drove out of the terminal hospital for the last time. I had been able to give a lot of prayer there but not the work of my ministry, and I could only think in my mind deep down, 'Father, I thank You'. You may wonder why my London hospital were so interested in me personally. I have been their patient for fourteen years and still am.

In the early days my back consultant asked if I would give my body after death to the hospital. I did so willingly and signed all the necessary papers. He was a marvellous man, very clever, and we had a good relationship, as I still have with all who look after me there. He used to tease me about my kind of religious life before the students—he always got everything wrong, but it caused good laughter. Later on, when I began to get more diseases, he started asking me real Christian questions, and I gave the answers.

Almost as soon as I went to live nearer the hospital and my kidney trouble had shown itself, he died of cancer in eighteen days. Before this it was not even suspected that he had it. When I heard about the trouble I wrote to him, and he answered but knew only a miracle could save him. Next time I went to my hospital I enquired from the chaplain about this consultant's 'passing'. He told me he had suffered very much, but before he died he did all the Christian things he should have done, and told the chaplain it was due to me and what I had told him in answer to his questions, and my own attitude towards illness. May God bless and accept that man's soul. I feel sure He has done.

My life soon became normal again once I arrived at my new home. True, it was not the anchorage and all pertaining to it. But it was the next best thing and the house has an atmosphere; because my room is cut off from the rest of the house by the little lobby it is quiet and there is always someone in the house if I need them because of illness, triggered off possibly from the first early illness and the kidney trouble. It is necessary to be mostly in bed now, and I do suffer very much pain. But God has taught me what to do with it. Also I can work my ministry from here.

I never left off my prayer life during the previous two and a half unhappy years. If one practises Infused Contemplation and Infused Recollection which are habitual, then prayer doesn't stop. It was my ministry that I could not carry on before. I felt that that period was God's testing of my trust in Him. After all, had He not captured me Himself and led me all the way? But the test had to come before He moved me on in the way He wished me to go.

I had now a very great impulse to pray to God direct. I seemed to be so close to Him and really felt inwardly that He was my Creator and my Father Spirit. Very humbly I say that somehow I felt the need to pray direct to God and not first to Christ. Also long before, I had felt the need to give up venerating relics when I was still at Walsingham. The saints are all so near to me, and this nearness seemed to override any kind of veneration. To me veneration seemed less appropriate than the actual nearness I felt. It also seemed to me that one cannot separate any part of the Church; the living and the dead are not separated in my mind. Both go to make up the whole Church and the 'Body of Christ'.

I spoke to my director about this and he told me, if I obtained no help from venerating saints' relics, to give it up. This I did. I also mentioned to him my problems of praying direct to God, that I had a force compelling me to do so, and I was already doing it. My director told me it was quite all right to pray to God direct providing I used 'through Christ' somewhere in the prayer or at the end. This I have been doing ever since.

St John the Baptist said of himself, 'I must decrease and He must increase'. This of course was alluding to Christ. To me it is the same kind of thing, only it is God who must increase and the humanity of Christ must decrease but the divine Christ must always remain the link.

This seemed to be confirmed in a way, because after arriving at my new home in Worcester, the 'voice' wakened me again and said, 'Love Me and all people, I am in them'. I crossed myself and it was repeated.

I have always loved people and animals, and find it easy to make animals do things. For instance, in my very early days, long before I saw my mountains, I could make a horse lie down gently and make it get up just as gently. I would never condemn people, however bad they were; they are God's creation and I still see them all as 'souls' and precious.

It is wonderful to be in a place where I can carry on my ministry in full again, and to be able to use the spiritual love deep down inside me. Not that I have ever lost this even during the two and a half most unhappy years. My interior never once lost sight of my Creator or stopped my interior prayer life. Now I felt at peace, even though illness had increased and still is increasing. But even this does not worry me. Little did I know what my Creator had in store for me.

> His eye sees every precious thing,
> He brings it forth to light;
> Father I thank You.

A DIFFERENT KIND OF LADDER
Sweet is the grape,
but sweeter when turned into wine

MY HOSPITAL decided I should come to them from Worcester twice a year, April and October, or in an emergency. I go lying full length on the back seat of a car and this arrangement works very well.

One of the things an Anchoress is allowed is a cat! Having obtained permission from my benefactress I started going into the matter. I knew exactly what I wanted but in the early stages of correspondence with a breeder I became ill, or rather more ill. Influenza was about in the town, and at the beginning I did not bother my GP, but about midweek I realised it was not influenza but kidney trouble. I could always tell by the performance of my temperature. A kidney temperature is unique and well did I know it! When I tried to contact my GP he was away on a course and short of phoning my London hospital myself it meant waiting until my GP's return. I became much worse but although the state of health deteriorated, I put my hand into the hand of my Creator and trusted.

As soon as my GP came back he found me in a rather sorry state. He contacted London immediately and I was rushed up as an emergency. My prayer life, although weary, never stopped, even though it may not have been of quite the usual quality. I was not worried because I knew that God knew what he was doing with me. The car driver is very good and I always have the same one every time. We arrived at my London hospital in just under three hours.

I was put in a side ward, and very soon the kidney team, except my consultant who was away at the time, were with me, led by his second in command. Oh! how true, God had me completely in His hands.

I had had no drugs since leaving home; it was now evening and I was in a fairly bad way having been ill already for a week, but I was quite conscious and had no drugs in the hospital as they first wanted to find out and be sure of the cause. I knew the doctors were talking with each other and the Sister at the bottom of my bed, but their voices seemed so far away, so very far away, something quite unnatural. One whom I knew very well came to my head and said, 'Are you all right?' I replied in a whisper, 'Yes, thank you. Am I going to die? I want to know, please'. He gave me an answer which I must keep secret as it was too precious to put into print. He left the hospital several years ago.

I had often told my director that it was my wish that God would strip me bare of all that displeased Him, and my director answered, 'He will'. On this occasion I tried to pray. Previously it had always been possible to pray right up to the operating theatre ante-room, as premedication never works on me. This time, having no drugs and not going to the operating theatre, I simply could not pray. I tried desperately hard, but could not do so. I could not even in thought or word utter one single thing. I knew what I wanted to pray but it simply would not come to the top of my interior. I seemed to be stripped bare of every single thing and felt a nakedness inside. All I wanted to do then, was to crawl to the Sacred Feet. This inwardly, I seemed to do. I saw them and the nail holes, and when this last thing happened I seemed to bow even lower than the crawl until my forehead touched the ground. Then I fell asleep. Later on when I thought about this 'happening', it made me understand in some small way how Christ's human nature must have felt on the Cross, and also that one could not even raise one's finger if it was not God's will.

I woke next morning to find I was very much better. Sister came in to see me, and from the bottom of the bed asked how I was and then said, 'You look as if you have been through it'. I replied, 'Yes, but I seem to have had the worst part of the illness at home!'

Apparently something inside had become lodged where it should not be, and during the night had moved of its own accord. I thought much on what had happened. 'Oh! my Father, You have allowed me to feel what it is like to be stripped bare of every possible earthly thing. Stripped bare so that I was not able even to pray. You have allowed me to feel what it is like when one's 'passing' comes when conscious. You have shown me more and more what I am against Your purity, my humility and weakness against Your strength. I am absolutely nothing, not even a speck of sand against Your feet, and yet You love me and are still going to use me as Your tool on earth through whom Your Holy Spirit may work Your will for others. Oh! my Creator give me the grace of strength and wisdom to be a good tool in Your sight.'

After a few days I was moved into the main ward and asked the Sister if I might have my communion. This was given and I offered thanks to God for all that had happened.

I decided not to have my curtains drawn during

communion and the chaplain did not mind. My idea was that others would see and perhaps feel they at some point would return to their communion. This worked. A patient came over to me during the day and said she had not had communion for twenty years and could she please join me next time I had it, to which I replied, 'Of course'. Then her friend came and told me she was not confirmed but could she come and just sit when her friend and I next received communion. Both of them came and the one that was confirmed received her communion with me while the other just remained quietly seated praying.

There was a lot of chatter in the ward about the curtains not being drawn, which was all very amusing. I understand that I started this not pulling round of the curtains as the chaplain told me later that it was happening in other wards.

There is a lot of fun to be had in hospital. I never mind going. I am off Rule for the period and do not wear a veil except at my communion, as that would ostracize me at once and probably keep other patients away from me. I am sure this is right. Quite a number of people who are up come to talk to me, and the inevitable question always comes, 'What do you do?' When I answer, 'I am a nun', they all almost fall under the bed! We all laugh a great deal, and when they find I am human, questions come very fast. I have been amazed at what some of these people think any kind of Christianity implies and I get asked many amusing questions. Hospital is a wonderful place for prayer; my intercession works overtime!

I have been in an L-shaped mixed ward many times and most patients seem to like it. The men do our early morning tea and sometimes the night drinks; it all seems to work very well. I get a number of slips of paper asking for prayers for something, from both men and women. With my infused prayer it is possible for me to continue to pray inwardly and talk with these people at the same time. It cannot be stressed too strongly that acceptance of illness is the key to happiness in illness, and I try to tell this to the patients who come to me and ask, 'Why should this happen to me?' I try to show them how to use their illness for others.

The one thing I will never do to anyone is to try to convert them. I will only answer their questions about religion if they ask me. It is up to them to use or not to use my answers. Also, outwardly I never talk about religion unless somebody asks me. I am sure these patients get a very different picture of what a nun is like from their preconceived ideas.

There are two things a nun must have, especially if God leads her to get involved with people. One is a quiet humour that people can see. Secondly an inward piety that other people cannot see. People have written to me about such piety, and have openly said that an obvious piety is offputting. Piety there must be, but it must be an inward piety, kept for when one is alone. Nuns are human and piety should be in that inward relation between God and the individual. I have found that, if a nun has these two qualities, people don't shun her. People who have endless troubles and are even seeking some kind of guidance, are more likely to write about them or even come for an interview.

When I first became a nun, and later when they knew I was becoming an Anchoress, many people wrote to me trying to dissuade me, and telling me how stupid I was. Now their attitudes are quite different. At the time, I told them that God Himself seemed to be leading me and I was only doing what my director and my bishop and I felt was God's will for me. How glad I am that I did not listen to them.

When I had been at Worcester a short while the correspondence was resumed with the breeder of my kitten. This had all been held up because of my sudden illness. The breeders brought two kittens for me to see, a boy and a girl, both blue Burmese. They were put on the bottom of my bed while everyone remained out of sight. I called them both and 'she' came up the bed to me. 'He' stayed where he was. So 'she' became 'Shan', and was taken back to her home to be neutered and brought back to me a week later. Shan was blessed at my next communion, and for ever after has lain quite quiet by my side when I have communion. She has learned to cross her paws every morning while I say an Our Father for her, and she also puts five pence on my little altar for her church collection.

It will perhaps be noticed that as I have progressed in my prayer life the voice has come less with longer intervals between and the visions have stopped. Since being in Worcester, the last voice I heard was in 1976. It wakened me earlier than ever before at 10.30 p.m. where previously it had always been in the early morning, and just said, 'Pray'. I crossed myself as always and it was repeated so I answered, 'What for Lord?' Immediately the answer came back, 'For this sick world'.

It seems to me that God has now the complete whole of me, made firm by the testing and trusting. He had made me completely ready for what was to come. I feel much spiritual sorrow both with the world, the Church, and of course, people. I can feel the hurt not only of the behaviour of the peoples of the world we live in, but also how all hurts God more than we can ever know.

> Oh my Father, through Your mercy
> I have been allowed the wine of the grape.
> I thank You, and offer myself again
> To be involved in whatever is Your wish and Your will,
> For I know You will show me.

INVOLVEMENT OF A DIFFERENT KIND
All people are God's children; love them

I ALWAYS take a weekly Christian paper. Sometimes it has an interview with some person of interest. Three different interviews have been done by me, but people did not know my name as I always write using a nom-de-plume. None of the questions pleased me very much because they were written questions and the answers were limited to a certain number of words and basically they were too superficial. So I asked to be interviewed 'off the cuff' as I much prefer to be questioned that way, but it was not permitted.

    The interviewer came to the house alone twice and once with a BBC technician to tape the interview. The questions I was asked were again not nearly searching enough, and frankly I did not want to do any of the interviews, because unless they were sufficiently probing they seemed to me rather a waste of time. I decided that never again would I do any interview from written questions, especially when one's answers are limited to a number of words.

The BBC promised to let me know when the recording was to be broadcast and I believe they did notify someone. But I did not get the message until after 4 p.m. on a Saturday that the broadcast would be on the following Sunday evening. There was therefore no time to notify my friends—also I was in hospital. The ward Sister took the message and gave it to me. I told no one in hospital and put my head under the bed clothes while the broadcast was on! After listening to remarks it seemed to have been received well, but I did not reveal myself. Although I did not like what I had done, God knew what He was doing and as it turned out this proved to be the starting point of new work and of involvement with others.

The paper for whom I did the interviews gave twenty free copies of each issue containing the interview. All these I sent to people I knew abroad. This brought me thousands of letters both directly and through the paper and interviewer. When I replied I gave my permanent address, still using my nom-de-plume. Here undoubtedly, was God's new work for me. All kinds of people wrote to me about their troubles, not only those concerned with a spiritual goal which many were desperately seeking, but also personal problems: marriage, work. There were letters on many subjects, but most were from people seeking a faith, or how to cope with illness.

Some of the people who wrote to me were priests. It was through correspondence with a priest that I came to know how retired single priests living in one of the clergy homes find it so difficult to settle. They have been used to ordering their own lives; then, when retirement comes and their only refuge is a priests' home, they find their lives organised for them. Some priests find this very hard to get used to.

I never answer these letters at once. I pray about each

case and ask God's Holy Spirit to answer through me; then when I am sure of what I should say, I write to them. The Holy Spirit must have time to work through me as the answers are from God, and I am only the 'tool' whom he uses for the purpose.

People of many religions write to me; some have no faith at all, others partly practice their own. This made me feel the need to be familiar with others types of religions, and I studied many. At the end of my study I came back to the point that God had shown me some time before, and that is that nearly all religions worship the same God, only in a different way. God has also shown me very clearly that we are all brothers and sisters right back to the start of the human race. I believe that and feel it. Illuminations from God have made this very clear to me, and this is why I suffer so much with people who both are receivers of some kind of hurt and also those who inflict the hurt. I also feel the joy of others in the same way. If I can feel it, how much more can God in Christ feel it? Mine can only be a pin-prick with infinitely divine feeling.

Some months later, television wanted to record an interview and the television people, including the director, came to my room. This time the interview was off the cuff but, oh dear! I was again to be disappointed. The lady did not seem to know what to ask me, and with my infused contemplation and habitual recollection, I prayed at the time that things might improve. But no, it was not to be. I later found out that it was her first attempt at interviewing. The short film when shown was not too bad, but I think my beautiful Burmese cat stole the picture! My friends knew who it was because of her.

This brought me thousands more letters and set the seal on what can be called a kind of spiritual 'help me' bureau which in a way has started, and increased, by telephone calls. I have four sets of people to deal with: those who stop writing after they get my one reply that

God inspires, those who keep on writing many times because they wish to become better and better, those whom I myself keep on my books because I know they cannot yet stand alone (these include many hundreds), and those who, if they are within possible distance and I know cannot be helped by letter, come to see me if possible. When any from either of the last two groups are ready, I try to pass them on to a good priest. So these numbers fluctuate, but always number hundreds.

Another way God's work snowballs is that my letters are often shown to others by the people who receive them, and then another lot starts up. Thus I always have to remember that I never know who is going to see my letter the other end. I am perfectly sure that these letters are the work of God going out through me, by the means of His Holy Spirit. I take no credit for them at all. I live so close to God and He must have the credit, for it is His work. Out of all the thousands of letters I have had, many more from abroad than England, I have only had letters from three people that I have been guided by God Himself not to help. These people I just answered politely, having no further correspondence.

This involvement with people arising from these radio and TV interviews, and even telephone conversations, has turned out to be the new work God had for me to do. As a result of this new ministry, I have become more and more involved with poor, spiritually sick and troubled people, and the guidance of God as to how to deal with them. I can see the pattern of my past secular life coming into the present work. Knowledge of a country and its people enables one to understand their troubles so much better. Although I have always loved people, this new involvement has made me love even the worst of them more, and taken my work to people all over the world, sometimes through the United Nations and the World Council of Churches in Geneva, to Arabia and many others, even the Philippines.

Of the people I have dealt with some have made enormous strides very quickly, some more slowly, and I have only had three that I would call failures, more or less, because they cannot somehow have a faith in anything, or have slipped back through lack of perseverance.

I have been asked a very great deal about death. I have met people who wish to know much about it, people who are afraid, people who do not believe in an afterlife and people who believe in reincarnation. I have faced death five times and God has taught me a great deal about it, and by doing so has equipped me to help these people. I myself have no fear of death.

It is the same with pain. Pain must be used for others and for the world as a whole. It is also true that pain once accepted must be used for others as our Lord used His. In this context it is possible to bear increasing pain and suffering as life proceeds. I know that if I had as much pain in the early days as I have now, I could not have borne it.

This chapter is being written on the Feast of the Transfiguration. This is one of my favourite feasts for does it not tell us so much, especially about life after death? First, the whiteness of Christ is made by the shadow of God reflected in Christ's humanity. This reveals to us, for a moment, the divinity of Christ. We know it was no ordinary whiteness because the three disciples Peter, James, and John, were bowed to the ground by it, and they did not know what to say. What they did say was so feeble (Matt. 17.1-10). They were so overcome. When light turns to whiteness it means it is not ordinary light but something greater and infinitely divine. We read also that Moses and Elijah reflected the whiteness. But to me the importance is in the fact that Moses died on earth and nobody knows actually where he is buried. Elijah was taken to heaven by the hand of God, so both souls went on in a different way, and here they were, both transformed into spiritual forms standing there with Christ in the middle reflecting God's divine self one by the other and all talking to each other. Does not this tell us much about the afterlife? I believe it shows us a great deal. It must also surely show us that we shall know each other in our spiritual state, and that there is another life after our departure from this world and our present finite state. St Peter mentions this vision several times in his writings; he never forgot it.

I never had any idea that God was going to lead me into so much involvement with many thousands of people worldwide. I knew He had brought me through that very bad illness for some reason, but did not know what. The work has been so rewarding; all my thanks, praise, and worship given to God seems no better than a grain of sand. More than ever I am only His tool through whom He works and all the credit goes to Him. He is the worker and I am very much an unworthy, very small tool.

Since I have been given this new work my Rule has had to be changed both to cope with my work and my illness. This has not been hard to adjust to because one grows out of parts of the Rule as progress in prayer life develops, and I am now to work as the Spirit of God shows. The basic things like my vows and praying of the Canonical Hours remain the same. I do not now have a warden as he became no longer necessary. I have my bishop who has appointed a very holy priest to come and administer my Holy Communion and to be responsible for any small things I may wish to ask. This all works very well. But all the credit for any work I do must go to God. He has accepted my whole life.

Sometimes, when I have very difficult clients and I might be worried about them, a very strong thought about their personal progress comes to me. They may be needing help in some way, even if I have written to them two or three weeks before. My wondering whether they are all right will not leave me for long. What happens? I suddenly get a telephone call from them and they are always in trouble, or need advice quickly.

Sometimes I become extra tired, just as if I am absolutely drained, quite unlike any ordinary tiredness and I fall asleep for maybe a quarter of an hour. At the time it feels as if I've suddenly lost all my energy. Then, in a day or two, sometimes I get a letter from one of my clients and, among other things in the letter, there will be a sentence, 'I was kneeling at prayer and I felt you were kneeling beside me; I knew you were there and I received much help.' When I check up the date of the letter, and the time of the other person's prayer, either morning or afternoon, it is found to be at the same time that I have been overcome with this absolute draining of my strength. I do not have it regularly, and I have not at the time been thinking of the person. But more than one person has told me this.

Of course I used to discuss these things with my director. Might the first be a kind of telepathy? But it is still left as a query. No decision can yet be given on the second, chiefly because I am not touching the people who seem to feel me beside them. The people who have written to me about this are people who have made great headway into contemplative prayer. These letters always arrive the following day but I have never told them of this draining experience. So at present these two kinds of phenomenon remain unsolved. If it is a draining out to someone, I have no knowledge who the person is until I receive the letter.

> Oh! My God and Creator,
> You have now led me into new paths of my life,
> All credit is to You.
> Grant that if it be Your will
> I may have continued strength and wisdom to do it.

JOY IS DEEPER THAN HAPPINESS
Spiritual love is God's nature in us.
Let us make it flow forth to others

NO ONE, whether secular or religious, should take a vow if in doubt about the ability to keep it. I mention this because, through the years and even these days, some secular people under their spiritual directors have sometimes made a vow of a kind. It may help some people but God tells us quite definitely not to make a vow unless it can be kept.

Let us look at the vows of the religious life. Obedience does not just mean obedience: it means obedience accepted at once outwardly either to the superior of a convent, or her representative; it means obedience to the bishop or his appointed warden. At the same time it also means obedience in the heart, mind, and thought. It is no use being obedient if your heart rebels.

The vow of poverty does not mean that you yourself are poor and living in poverty. Nearly all nuns have what is necessary, including good food. It means poverty of heart, mind, all one's senses and faculties. It does not mean that it is just something shown outwardly or on purpose; it is a deep, inner poverty touching self, and making one humble.

Chastity means a cleanliness of body, of senses and faculties, of heart and thought. There are many things to think about that work not only outwardly, but also in the mind and soul and making one both humble and pure in God's sight.

Secular people who order their lives according to a rule of life under directors, should not struggle to keep a rule they cannot manage. They should ask for the rule to be made easier so they can keep it in the world in which they live.

Through my various correspondence, I often get asked to whom the marriage vows are made. They are, of course, made to God, through the priest, and to each other if the marriage is in Church. I make my vows to God through my bishop by putting my hands between his while I am saying the words. Because of my special branch in the religious life I have five vows, perpetual life vows.

God has given me a great deal of enlightenment concerning the New Testament. I first studied St Matthew's Gospel. The first thing I noticed was that the four Gospels are called 'The Gospel according to St Matthew, Mark, Luke and John.' With the exception of St John, God also showed me that we cannot be sure the first three Gospels were written by the authors named; they may have been written by others. But with St John's Gospel, St John never mentions his name. He writes calling himself 'the disciple whom Jesus loved'. This Gospel is the youngest and probably written near the end of the last decade of the first century, about AD 90–100, or earlier. But St John writes naming himself as Jesus' special disciple, and it would appear that he did in fact write it himself. Each Gospel tells different things about Our Lord's work on earth and by reading them carefully, together with commentaries as companions to the texts, we can understand different aspects of Christ's life.

St John was a mystic and writes as such not only of himself but also of Christ, in order to show people the divine side of Christ's life. Christ tells us we are to love our neighbour as ourselves. Of course, a person cannot love everybody. We are finite human beings, and as such we all have our faults. But we can do something about loving our neighbour even if we don't want to. I was praying about this once, as I had someone I just could not love wholeheartedly, and the illumination came to me, 'Yes, you can love this person'. (By that love I mean spiritual love, not temporal love.) 'You can put the person very high in prayer.' I asked my director about this and he confirmed that that was the right thing to do.

There is another subject of which I have had illumination through prayer. After Christ had risen, Mary Magdalene was weeping outside the tomb, and she did not recognise Christ at once when he spoke and thought He was the gardener; but when Christ spoke her name, 'Mary', she recognised Him at once and went to touch Him. But He would not let her. People often wonder why. It appears to me that Mary Magdalene was still too much in her earthly state. She was still thinking in earthly terms of her beloved as she had always done. She had not yet come to know the risen Christ. She was not yet ready or did not understand enough to put away her temporal self and realise the divine. She was not yet ready to understand that the human Christ before the crucifixion was the divine Christ after He had risen. Mary was still earthly and imperfect.

People often ask me about the resurrection and I write here what has been given to me by prayer. Christ had the power according to both natures, human and divine, while on earth. After the crucifixion, His glorified body became submissive to His glorified soul, and so the body was under the control of the Spirit and He rose by divine power. In his lifetime, Christ seldom used His divine power, nearly always His human power, being the highest force of His nature. But after the crucifixion there was only the divine power left in control. This is also why He would not let Mary Magdalene touch him; she was still only human and could not be allowed to touch the divine. This has been shown to me very clearly in prayer, and I have no doubt that for me, this is the truth.

I get a tremendous amount of support and inspiration from certain books and pieces of music. It would be impossible to list all these, and it is up to everyone to find one's own. But I would like to mention a few examples for those who are not sure where to look, or who would like something to be recommended.

Some valuable books are: *The Dream of Gerontius* by Cardinal Newman, *Hymn of the Universe* by Teilhard de Chardin, and the writings of St John of the Cross. Certain music can be a very helpful aid to devotion and prayer. I particularly enjoy and am inspired by: *The Four Seasons* by Vivaldi, and any Beethoven piano music particularly when played by Vladimir Ashkenazy.

I have been amazed at the number of people, both men and women, who are desperately seeking a faith of some kind. So many times the answers to my letters come back, 'I never knew, it seems so easy when put like that'. People like things simple these days and anyone can pray, even in the hubbub of this present age. Prayer is always easy if one understands it. It should never be difficult and it should be short rather than long.

We are often told that the Church is dying or that England is no longer a Christian country. This is very wrong. It may not be seen to flourish but a Christian country it still is, make no mistake about that.

I have often been asked whether I would condemn anyone, even a murderer. My answer is no. I would not condemn anyone, only God knows the heart of a person and He is the judge. Also, I believe a murderer is just as much my brother as anyone else, because he or she may change. They make me suffer, very much, but I believe at some point they will get their chance to reform. I also believe it is only those rejecting God at the very end of the Last Judgement whom God will reject. And even in that He is merciful, for a person still rejecting God at the last moment, having seen Him in glory, would have hell living with God in a heavenly state everlastingly.

People also ask if I ever try to convert people. I answer their questions or try to comfort them in times of trouble, and I always tell people to take from my letters anything they find useful and forget and throw away what is no use to them, but I never make a conscious effort to convert a correspondent.

Sometimes I get very distressed letters from mothers who have a mentally disturbed child. Perhaps the family is Christian, and they are in despair because the mentally disturbed child cannot learn the faith. I say to all those families of any religion, be kind and gentle to them and remember that because of their condition, they cannot sin.

I shall carry on my present work, until either God gives His tool new work or calls me through illness to Himself.

The best beauty is always at the top of the mountain.
FATHER, I THANK YOU

EXISTENCE OF FREEDOM
You shall know the truth
and the truth shall make you free

SO NOW we come to the end of this particular spiritual life and must take stock of all that has happened in the past twenty-seven years. Even though I had very little religious background, except formal Baptism and Confirmation which at the time meant nothing to me, and even missed God's call when it came in the early days, this could have been God's will; I was not ready for it. I am fairly certain that it was a call but I failed to recognise it. When the voice came back to me so vividly in later years, exactly the same voice, I still never felt any inclination to be a nun. It was my first director who found that out when I was a novice. I did not feel it was right, and my director, when he said it might be a higher vocation, confirmed this. I would never have had all the experience and benefits of travel, which have been so very useful in my present life, had I heeded the first call.

Is the discipline of training in preparation for the life

of an Anchoress necessary? I say most firmly, 'yes'. Does it need to take such a long time? Again I say, 'yes'.

We are so full of ourselves; the training is necessary, not only to reveal our own faults and so get rid of them, but to learn to be pliable in God's hands so that He can work through us by means of His Holy Spirit. Once all the unnecessary things have been pruned away, then the work of God starts to happen, and the more open one is to God, the more He can work in us, His works not ours.

I have said that the nine and a half years in my Anchorage at Walsingham were the happiest of my life. That is true, and my memorial brick is in the wall facing the high altar, there for all to see; except for illness I should be there today. It is also true that the time I was in the terminal hospital was the unhappiest in my life.

When one is so completely given to God, life in itself is so happy. One is not worried about anything, one does the work God gives. He may change it or He may not. I have had the same bishop for twenty-two years. I saw him in 1976 and said to him, 'Oh, my Lord, I am so very happy, so very, very happy, even though I am ill'. He paused for a moment, then turned to me and said very quietly, 'You look like that, you really do'. I could only repeat that I was.

My bishop and I have had a most wonderful working partnership. He is such a holy man, so full of humility and wisdom, and he is still my bishop and will remain so until God separates us by His call.

Another thing that is so wonderful is the fact that when God blesses with both infused contemplation and infused habitual recollection, one not only puts into action St Paul's words 'pray without ceasing'; one gets into a holy indifference to the things of earth that are material. For instance I am in bed nearly all the time and I am allowed certain things like plants (I grow bonsai trees) because I cannot go into the garden and work. I have certain things necessary for my illness, one being a cold fan. I have everything that is necessary for my work and other things, because my life is so concentrated in one room. Most nuns have all that is necessary for them, but they have to ask when they want these things. I, not having a community, have different things written into my Rule, with the exception of things for health which I need anyway. But the fact that I have a 'holy indifference' to it all, makes all the difference.

If someone came into my room and said, 'I am going to take all your plants away', I would not mind one little bit. My first director made that very clear one Christmas when I was at Walsingham. The late administrator brought me a Christmas present of a tiny bottle of Cointreau, a liqueur of which I am very fond and I had tasted none since the war. I thanked him. I looked at it and thought: Shall I open it or not? This was in the early days of my Anchoress life and I kept this up for half a day! Then someone else came to give me Christmas wishes so I gave her the little bottle I so wanted to open. When my director came next time, I told him about the little bottle. He said at once, 'You silly thing, you should have opened it and enjoyed it. Take what God gives you and be thankful, but don't long for another'.

When I heard the voice in later years, it made me wonder very much for a few moments if I had indeed missed the call earlier because it was exactly the same tone. I never allow these things to linger in my mind, also I never talk about them. When I have the answers, I just keep a mental account of them and put them deep away inside. They have never been mentioned before this book. These things are so precious one feels one must keep them secret. They are far too precious to talk about.

The closer one gets to God makes one's life freer. If I have a personal problem, I put the whole thing into the hands of God and, instead of worrying about it, I just wait for God's answer. It always comes, maybe not in the way I expect it, but it comes. Because I am so given to God, I know He will take care of me because He knows already before I tell Him about it. Indeed, I have just had a problem and He provided the answer, in His own good time.

So you see I live in freedom. It is very easy to exist, but look what worry people have who do just exist, either with or without any faith. So many people do just that. They beat the air so often with open hands and worry in times when that is so much trouble anyway. I was only existing in my early life and this could not be compared with freedom. Yes, I have had both, and what of me now? I am so quietly busy, so very happy, even with so many illnesses, but because of my loving and believing with utter trust in God, I am free. Yes, I have an abundant happiness and I am free.

> God in Christ has given me a deep inner knowledge of truth stored deep in my heart.
> Believe in truth, truth shall make you free, and instead of existence there is freedom.

THE OUR FATHER
arranged for the use of Intercession

LET US make an act of fellowship with all mankind through the prayer Our Lord commanded us to pray. Let us realise that it is only through the spirit of this prayer that our personal, social and international problems can ever be solved.

OUR FATHER WHO ART IN HEAVEN
We are always in the presence of God our Father, although we too often forget it. In using that name, we commit ourselves to the fact that He 'made of one blood all nations', and that every human being is God's creation, and our brothers and sisters. Let us try to grasp the one-ness of God's family in humanity.

Prayer
Our Father, grant that we may walk worthily of this glorious relationship. Teach us to realise the Eternal

Presence. Help us to believe that there is a power that can lift us into heavenly places. Teach us to worship you, not in fear, but with the reverence of true filial love. Expand the horizon of our minds and prayers, so that they may truly include the whole of mankind, the whole family of God.

HALLOWED BE YOUR NAME
Let us dwell on the infinite holiness and infinitely perfect love of God, and try to understand the demands this holiness and love make on our sinful nature and unloving lives. Let us plead to be made sensitive to what is beautiful, and responsive to what is good, not only in the world of nature, but in all our fellow men, so that it may be easier for others to see God through us.

Prayer
We praise You, we bless You, we worship You, we glorify You, we give thanks to You for Your great glory, O Lord God, heavenly King, God the Father Almighty ... Help us to show forth Your praise, not only with our lips but in our living, and in the treatment which we give to all Your creation. Grant us grace to walk before You in holiness and love, that our whole being may reflect Your goodness so that others may desire to find You and to worship.

YOUR KINGDOM COME, YOUR WILL BE DONE ON EARTH AS IT IS IN HEAVEN
Let us remember that as we pray for the Kingdom we must also work for it. Let us ask for grace not to hinder its coming by putting lesser things first in our own lives. Let us pray for a wider vision, for the leaders of the world, of nations, of individual states, that they may know God and work in obedience to His will of justice and peace, in integrity and wisdom.

Prayer
Grant, O Lord, that the rule of love may come to replace the rule of force throughout the world. Make all men builders of Your Kingdom by showing that the ideas of the Spirit can command our loyalty and can direct our lives here and now. Make us quick to see and ready to encourage all who would know You. Help us to conquer the forces of evil in ourselves that we may not hinder the coming of the Kingdom.

GIVE US THIS DAY OUR DAILY BREAD
Let us remember with thankfulness the gifts we so often take for granted, remembering others who are not so richly blessed. Let us plead for the spirit of willingness to share our good things with others who have not so many blessings, that none of us may go hungry in body, mind or spirit. Let us plead for the spirit of co-operation amongst all men, and for a deeper sympathy and understanding that recognises needs and tries to meet them.

Prayer
Our Father, we thank you for all Your providential care and the many blessings of our lives. We beseech You to look with mercy upon those who are hungry, sick, lonely, discouraged, or frustrated. We plead for quickened imagination and generous hearts, that we may seek to serve the common good, finding our true satisfaction in the well-being of others for the love of You.

FORGIVE US OUR TRESPASSES
AS WE FORGIVE THEM THAT TRESPASS
AGAINST US
Let us ask for patience and understanding with the faults of others and a stern watchfulness over our own. Let us keep our eyes fixed on the highest point of the cross,

keeping ourselves humble by our own failures and making us forgiving of the failures of others. Let us plead for forgiveness for all unjust judgements and criticisms passed on our fellow men, and for strength to offer restored fellowship to those who have wronged us.

Prayer
O God, Who by the Cross of Jesus has shown us how sin can be taken away by the love that offers full forgiveness, we acknowledge our sins known and unknown by which we have so often frustrated Your grace and high purposes, and we confess our full share in all the evils which hold back the coming of Your Kingdom. We beg Your forgiveness for all our attitudes of superiority, of lovelessness and intolerance, by which we have kept Your world small and divided.

LEAD US NOT INTO TEMPTATION BUT DELIVER US FROM EVIL

Let us ask that we should not go carelessly into temptation day by day, but that if temptation comes, we may be given insight to recognise it, and strength of spirit to meet it without fear, and grace to overcome it. Let us pray that we may not knowingly put temptation in the way of others or make it harder for them to resist it. Let us beseech our heavenly Father for a constant sense of His saving presence, so that at every moment of spiritual testing or moral danger, we may know and feel His power is available for us.

Prayer
O Holy God, Holy Immortal, holy and strong, Who looks not on appearance, but on the heart, have mercy upon us. Grant us delight in all that is of good report, and create in us a new heart and desire for moral good, that we may be delivered from our sins, and set free to do Your perfect

will. Grant that we may be a strength to others in their times of weakness.

FOR YOURS IS THE KINGDOM
THE POWER AND THE GLORY FOR EVER
Let us try to realise the boundless resources of God, not remote and limited, but near at hand for every need of every soul, and ALL creation.

Prayer
O Eternal Father, Father of compassion, Who has made us for Yourself, have mercy on us. We acknowledge our frailty and are not able to serve You worthily. The world is strong and we are weak. But You are ever watching to perform Your will in us, and through the merits of Jesus, Your strength is made perfect in weakness. Keep the vision of Your love and Your power and the guidance of the Holy Spirit ever before us, and as we come to see You more clearly, grant that we may come to love you with our whole being, and so love and serve all our brethren for Your sake.
Through Jesus Christ our Lord, Who with You and the Holy Spirit lives and reigns for ever, Amen.

SIMPLE PRAYER FOR PEOPLE IN A BUSY WORLD

THIS ARTICLE is not meant to probe into the many higher forms of prayer and contemplation, but perhaps it will help the ordinary soul living in the hurried pace of the present age.

All souls are made with God's nature and have, as it were, two parts. The surface which is all the earthly things we do and the temporal things we think and the depth, which is the interior which only God knows. It is the movement of this deep interior which makes us want to pray, the image in us seeking after the Image Creator, so to speak, and trying to communicate with It.

A soul that prays should have a deep devotion for the Trinity, Father, Son and Holy Spirit, because they must ALL come into prayer. The soul must look upon God as *a real Father*, not only as Creator. Secondly, a soul must realise its total dependence upon Him. Thirdly, each soul is God's special providence, and fourthly, He is the hidden ruler of every soul and master of its destiny. Out of these realisations comes love, not an emotional love but a deep lasting love for a loving Father, and even though He cannot be seen the soul *knows* Him to be there.

Now true perfect love is Uncreated Love, and this is the Holy Spirit dwelling in the heart, and it is the Holy Spirit Who teaches and moves a soul to pray. When the soul prays it is the Holy Spirit Who prays *in it*, because He too dwells in its heart and carries on, in the flame of His own love, our prayers through Jesus to the Father.

It is always difficult for the average person to have love for and devotion to someone Who is invisible, but if we give ourselves to the Holy Spirit and implore Him to work in us, just as we are, in all simplicity, the insight will come and with it love and devotion.

Having gained this how can we start our prayer? First of all, give glory to the Trinity, 'Glory be to Father, Son and Holy Spirit.' Then morning oblation is important. A soul must realise that God works *through* us all day in all things and daily oblation is so important.

> O my God, I offer to you this day all the work and all the joys, sorrows, the trials, tribulations, frustrations, health or sickness, my love and devotion, for the intention of the Sacred Heart in the Holy Sacrifice of Thy Passion.

That prayer embraces and sanctifies everything a soul does for the whole day, and everything done contributes to make life fruitful and turns action into prayer. All things become prayer as they happen or are done through the day, and it is not necessary to think any more about them. It is the attitude of oblation in all a soul does in accepting trouble, suffering, sickness, that has redemptive action. Oblation united to the passion of Christ *is* Christ penetrating *through* His mystical body, the Church. It is the Church with whom and through whom the soul offers oblation, and then lives it out through the day by actions and deeds, some active, some passive. What is so often said, that prayer is the lifting of the heart to God, is true and any fleeting thought of God, however small, is a lifting of the heart and a prayer through the prompting of the Holy Spirit.

It is not necessary to kneel to pray but it is necessary to be humble in spirit and realise the infinite greatness of the One to whom one is praying, and the littleness of oneself in comparison. One must always remember God is infinite and we are finite. Prayer should never be forced or hard. It should always be simple and easy. It need not be actual words at all.

If a soul truly loves God, it will keep God in the depths of its interior. In other words, God will enter into everything, into all the soul does, into all visible creation of nature. It will see Him *there* as the 'Master Hand', without which no soul could raise one finger, and nothing could exist, because the greatness of God is the principle of all motion, all life, of all intellectual and spiritual life, the source, foundation, root, and soul of all power and force outside Himself.

In this age of hurry and bustle, finding time is so difficult for the average person, but prayer can still continue. Here are some simple ways:

When washing your hands
    O Lord Jesus, through the merits of Thy passion
    Wash away my sins and those of all sinners.

When you are dressing
    Lord, I thank You for giving me these clothes,
    and I ask You to bless the people who made them.

When walking down a London street or some other
    O Eternal Father, I offer You
    the Precious Blood of Jesus

in reparation for all sinners
who walk on the other side of the street this day.

When riding in a bus
O Eternal Father, I offer You
the work of all London bus drivers this day
for their sins and all the wants of Holy Church,
through Christ our Lord.

For prisoners
O Lord Jesus, I offer You
all the work I do this day
as an act of reparation for all prisoners
under life sentence.

When washing up
O Lord Jesus, I offer this washing up to you
and ask You to perfect it for me and
offer it to the Father with Your own divine heart,
in reparation for the sin of the world.

When seeing someone in need or distress
Eternal Father, You know his (or her) needs,
help him according to Your will
through Jesus Christ.

When unlocking a door
O Holy Father, send Your Holy Spirit
into the hearts of all men,
that they may come to know and love You.

At the chiming of a clock
I pray for the recovery according to the Will of God,
for all people undergoing operations at this moment,
and I unite their sufferings to the Passion of Christ.

When passing someone
    Lord Jesus, have mercy on him (or her)
    and grant all his needs.

When listening to the news and a number of deaths are mentioned large or small
    O my God I offer You the Precious Blood of Jesus
    in reparation for their sins
    and all the wants of Holy Church.

When looking at a world watch
    Pray for the country the large hand is pointing to.

The word 'Father' said in the heart with love and devotion, is a prayer in itself.

So one can go on in a hundred and one ways all through the day with this ejaculatory prayer; one's life becomes a living prayer for the world, the Church, and one's fellowmen. The words need not be said aloud. They can be uttered in the heart. By joining all activity, whatever kind, with God together in prayer and in union with the cross of Christ, your life can become one living sacrifice for the sake of the whole world and the Church, the *whole* Church, and thereby partake in the work of redemption.

People often speak of 'private prayer', but really there is no such thing, because we pray as the Church. However hidden or apparently hidden such prayer may be, it is still the whole Church praying.

NIGHT LITANY

O GOD our Father hear us, through Your Son. We plead for all who tonight stand in most need of Your merciful love and protection.

Those who are tempting others,
those who are carrying on wicked trades,
those indulging in sinful amusement,
those who are imperilling themselves by self-indulgence,
all who are out tonight—the homeless, the weary, the
   starving, those tempted to suicide,
the intemperate.
    HAVE MERCY

Those who are out to rescue others.
    GRANT HELP AND PROTECTION

For those who work at night, the police, railwaymen,
   firemen, night watchmen, soldiers, sailors and airmen,

sentries, actors, editors, journalists, Members of Parliament, television and radio personalities
> YOUR PRESENCE BE WITH THEM

Those who this night must suffer bereavement,
The sick and the suffering, and all who are enduring any agony of mind or body, and all undergoing operations.
> HELP THEM IN BODY AND SOUL

The sleepless, the lonely, those in anxiety, nervous or mental distress, the insane.
> KEEP THEM IN YOUR POWER

Those who attend upon the insane, night nurses, priests and doctors called out in the night.
> REWARD THEM

Those whom sudden death summons before their judgement, those for whom this will be their last night on earth, those dying alone without Priest or Sacrament, those dying unconscious, those dying in any country and of any race who are near death, those trying to turn to Thee even in their last hour.
> RECEIVE THEM LORD HAVE MERCY

Those who are afraid to die, for dying priests and all communicants.
> RECEIVE THEM TO YOURSELF

The faithful departed of all races, for ourselves in our last hour.
> GRANT PARDON FOR OUR SIN, OUR NEGLIGENCES AND OUR IGNORANCE

For all addicted to drugs, and drug pushers, on behalf of those who have said no prayers today.
    FATHER, HELP THEM

On behalf of all those who blaspheme and neglect the Blessed Sacrament, let us say,
    BLESSED, PRAISED, HALLOWED, WORSHIPPED
    AND ADORED BE CHRIST, GOD OF ALL,
    WE BEG THY MERCY
    AMEN

THE RELIGIOUS LIFE

THERE MUST BE a true vocation to any branch of the religious life otherwise it would be hell for anyone. It is true that the clothes don't make the nun but my goodness, when one is invested after being a postulant, the clothes make all the difference in the world. They are all blessed by the bishop with the exception of the habit, (the postulant leaves the chapel to put on the habit which has already been blessed previously by the bishop and then returns to the chapel and kneels before the bishop in it). She already wears a small white veil which is changed before the bishop by other nuns for a larger white one which is worn by a novice.

MEANING OF THE CLOTHES:
  The Habit: The robe of Christ.
  Scapular: Three-quarter lengths for novices, long for fully professed and put on by the bishop. It is the symbol of obedience, the yoke of Christ.

The Girdle: The rope by which Christ was bound to the whipping post. Some communities have three knots, symbol of Christ and the two thieves; others have leather girdles without knots and some just have belts.

The Veil: Poverty and chastity.

The Crucifix: Dead to the world and alive to Christ.

The Headband: The cloth that bound Christ's head in the tomb.

The Wimple: The white robe or sheet that bound Christ in the tomb.

There are short prayers for each item as one puts it on.

A community should have a bishop who visits generally once in two or three years, interviews the Superior and questions her in the Counsels of the religious life. He also interviews each member in the community singly and does professions.

The community should have a constitution as well as a Rule. Chapters are held at intervals for anything special, for example, acceptance of a postulant, and then, when her time is up, whether she will go on to the noviceship or be dismissed by the chapter. She must have two thirds of the vote to stay and the Superior has a casting vote. The same thing happens when she is due for profession from the noviceship. If accepted for profession she is a 'junior' for three years. Noviceship varies with communities from three to five years. Voting is again taken at the end of her juniorship and then, and only then, does she become a fully professed nun and is no longer free to leave. At the same time all her possessions, including money, go to the community. These times may vary with different communities.

So you see, in Anglican communities it is a long time before one is fully in, and that rests with the community. One can leave at any time up until then.

EPILOGUE

TO ME it is quite clear that we have here and now no lasting state, but in Hebrews it says, 'But we seek a state that is to come' (13.14). I like to say we have no abiding state but we go towards a better everlasting state. I do believe heaven is a state to which one is called by God from this earthly life. We start making our future state during this life, so we are living in time and eternity together. It must be understood that God is spirit and that spirit is in everything and is everywhere. St John tells us, 'God is spirit and they who worship Him must worship in spirit and in truth'.

My first director once told me that when I could see the Spirit of God in a grain of sand my faith would be very firm. This I soon could do. Sand in some ways has been in my life a great deal, for I have been blown about like a grain of sand, hither and thither. I have camped in the desert and seen many sandwhirls, all the work of God. Now I have answered God's call, I take it that this blowing about of myself has been the Holy Spirit, but I did not recognise this forty years ago when seeing the first sand whirlwind.

No human being has ever converted me or directed me in any way. God Himself has done all and the people such as my bishop and director have, I think, recognised this; that is why they wait for me to ask whatever is necessary. I had to be blown about a very great deal, before I saw God in the Atlas Mountains, something that will remain with me all my earthly life.

It seems to me that God meant to have this little tool sometime, whatever happened. Do I regret the sacrifice? No, how can one regret anything if one has freedom and is free? One can be in the world but not of it. Let us all remember that this world is given to man on trust. Man has free will, a very dangerous and powerful weapon, because he can use it for good or evil. May everyone give some thought to this before it is too late.

Talk to God, Christ, or the Holy Spirit in your own way, anytime, and in your own words; they are so much better than other people's prayers from books, except the prayers of Holy Church, which should be used as they are written. In the name of God my Creator, His Son and Holy Spirit, I ask His blessing on every person of any kind or faith throughout the whole world. My prayers will continue for ALL of you. I mean it.

I am free with real freedom and can see the whole world in my mind as Christ could when He was tempted.

> Oh, eternal, merciful Father, Creator of all;
> the Spirit of life and Teacher of truth;
> by the power of the Holy Spirit,
> stir up the hearts of all men,
> that the world may again turn to You.
> O, compassionate Father,
> who has made us with Your nature,

who is at times making all things new,
grant us spiritual insight to know You
and to worship You,
so that we may come, at Your bidding
to our lasting state to share
united with You and one another,
eternal love forever,
through Christ Our Lord, *Amen.*

The Feast of the Transfiguration, 1978